G
"HELL
OUT OF YOUR
MARRIAGE

Christian Family Church and World Outreach Center
2300 Heritage Place NW | Owatonna, MN 55060
info@cfcmn.org | www.cfcchurches.org

Legacy Books

Table of Contents

Dedication

I have never believed in the phrase "self-made millionaire." It takes many touches from many people to see a goal to completion. It takes a team. I want to thank my "team".

Doug Sutcliffe, thank you for editing the pages that are about to be read. You are a true faithful friend.

Stephanie Merritt, thank you for typing these pages and even interpreting my handwriting! You are always a delight and joy to have in our staff and life. You are the best!

Danielle Zacharias, thank you for putting the manuscript "together" and sending it off to become a finished product. You make what you do look so easy. You are a huge blessing.

My long-time friend Mike Francen, thank you for helping me go from sitting with people in my office to expanding my counseling to a broader audience with a pen. You're a great encourager and writer. I'm honored that such an accomplished author gave me so much time and talent.

My mother Joyce LaFavre for editing as well, but most of all for always encouraging me with loving affirmations. I love you.

My father Jerry LaFavre who has, like my mother, been a loud cheerleader to me in all that I've done. Thank you, Dad. I love you.

My children, Trey, Stephany, Rachelle, Chantel, and Trom for cheering me on and believing in their mother. I love you.

Finally, to my amazing husband Tim (aka "my man"). I have many titles, but my favorite has always been Mrs. Tim Peterson. Thank you for begging me to marry you just after three weeks. At least that is how I like to remember it.

Even in our beginning days when we only had a little house and a whole lot of love, it was easy for me to see the greatness in you! I really do know who I married. Thank you for protecting my security. Thank you for being the strong and steady tortoise in the race of life. Thank you for not rolling the dice on my security even when opportunities came along. And thank you for putting Jesus first, family second, and then ministry. It has paid off.

I love you with all my heart.

Preface

A number of years ago I had a dream. In my dream I had this thought of going to my website. I remember thinking… "I have a website?" So, I went to my computer and looked up cherriepeterson.com. To my surprise…I did, I actually had a website!

At this site an invoice came up on the screen. It was a typical sales invoice. It had quantity and title of books, price/unit, and total.

I was able to see at least three book titles. So here is the second on the list!

- Cherrié Peterson

Introduction

It is clear that marriage today is highly UNDERRATED and a lost art. I believe marriage is meant to be a source of great strength in your life. It is meant to be an empowerment for success and not for weakness or adversity.

It's true, great marriages happen intentionally. It's true, when two people both agree that it's their goal to learn and keep learning how to be a great spouse, the results will be a great marriage.

This book is a manual of how to have a great marriage and truly get the *Hell* out of your Marriage.

\- Pastor Cherrié Peterson

CHAPTER 1

Redefining Hell

Let's take a moment to bring yet another definition of 'hell'. I am sure you have your own idea and concept of 'hell', and some define it as the condition of your current marital relationship, but it was never meant to be 'normal' in any relationship, especially the marriage union.

It is interesting to me that when two people come together in their nuptials and say, "I Do", they soon come from two different forms of 'normal'.

Before I met Tim, I had never heard of 'Lefsa'. (For those of you who may not know either, Lefsa is Norwegian flat bread.) Tim's family always had this Scandinavian specialty on their Thanksgiving and Christmas dinner tables. Arrayed with butter and brown sugar, it was a slice of heaven. It was a new tradition for me, but one I found easy to adopt as one of my favorites.

My family, on the other hand, always had the candy 'Divinity', delivered by my Swedish grandmother, and no one could imagine a holiday table not garnished with this treat. This was something new and foreign to Tim at our holiday feasts.

When it comes to 'relationships' you will be introduced to fun and delectable 'normals', and sometimes some 'normals' that are not as palatable. How people deal with hurts, anger, voice opinions, and even judgments are 'normal' to people in different ways. While some families, when an offense may arise, go straight to the offender and talk it through with them, others' 'normal' may be to go and share the offense with everyone else, thus creating drama.

I encourage couples in realizing they come from two different worlds, trying to blend them together and to create their own style of 'normal.' **This process must be done with a light heart and hopefully a sense of humor. I promise this makes the recipe in creating their own 'normal' much easier.**

In the upcoming pages I will divulge some of the differences between Tim and myself and our own path of discovering and creating what has become a 'normal' for our family. Neither Tim or I grew up in a family that knew how to communicate well; however, through his passion for pastoring, Tim quickly learned the importance of good Godly communication.

As for me, I was a 'stuffer' in order to keep anyone from getting upset. I simply tried to keep peace and express kindness and offer help. I just did not want to create hurts or stress; therefore, I never developed the skill of how to express my feelings. So I 'stuffed' them… until I couldn't any longer! Yikes!

For the first couple years of our marriage, about every six months, I would have an 'UNSTUFFING'! It was a real and unappealing action, but it was real. I would explode and want to run and escape. Tim often had no idea of the 'stuffing' that had overloaded me, but every six months or so he would certainly find out. I just wanted to run.

We all carry some kind of 'hell' from our past that just doesn't work in present days or future relationships. **This act of 'stuffing' was my 'hell.'** There are many forms of 'hell' that people carry that just won't work long term. These forms of 'hell' are not capable to form the actions or feelings that will make your marriage stronger. In actuality, the opposite often occurs. Its greediness divides you, and that 'hell' can eventually completely pull your marriage apart.

One way to describe 'hell' is clearly your 'uglies'. (Yes, I made up the word, but you get it.) Our 'uglies' are what we know they are. They stand forth as our own immaturities. They spring forth as our own immaturities, temperaments, tantrums, guilt, shame, and can force a God-ordained marriage into subsequent divorce. Horrible words are spoken out of anger – meaningless discrepancies in our own immature nature – because we are not versed in how to handle such. It just does not work! This is vital to remember and learn how to handle.

Such ambitions and endeavors will never take you into the marriage union you have been ordained to have. This conditional selfish love is comprised of each other's 'hell'. It is high time to 'GET THE HELL OUT OF YOUR MARRIAGE'.

When our four children were young, I noticed each one of the 'uglies' that arose. It is human nature. The same holds true in your marriage union. My heart is to help you put aside any and all of the 'uglies' (hell) and any immaturities so you can have the God-ordained and incredible marriage you always dreamed of – the marriage God intended.

CHAPTER 2

Forbearance

Not long ago I was on my way from our Minneapolis campus, and Tim was on his way home from our campus an hour south. We decided to meet at Chipotle's for dinner. A good friend of ours also joined us. As we were in the line, I happened to receive a text. It was from a couple that seem to always ask for much more than they give. Ok, they are big takers!

Tim is always on protective mode concerning my time and energy. He asked what they wanted, and I told him. He wanted to make sure that I didn't let them "run all over me." I told him I knew what to do, and he just kept talking to me and telling me how to handle it. I let him know that I know what to do and would just like to relax and order my food. He was silent for a minute and then just kept going. I said, "Honey, I know what to do and I just want to relax and have dinner together."

Tim paid, we got our drinks, and after a full day of counseling I was ready to relax and enjoy my meal. Tim, however, started up again and wanted to know what I had planned to say to this couple. I then looked at him and said, "Honey, even my taste buds are mad at you right now!" Our friend laughed and my man got the point!

The Bible talks about forbearance. I also am known to look at my man and tell him that I'm heading towards forbearance with him. What does this mean? It means that I'm upset and want to use words to tell him versus emotions. The Bible is clear that we are to walk in love, and EVEN when we disagree, we can be honoring and loving to each other. This is vital for a loving and healthy relationship.

Couples fall in love through words of love and kindness and get divorced because of words and unkindness. I'm a firm believer that we can all use words versus our emotions when we disagree. We can still be respectful and honoring to each other when we do not agree. We are to be protectors of each other's heart as we grow together. It is vital to even be kind when we disagree!

It's a reality that couples will have disagreements. However, we are the ones that get to choose how we are going to handle our disagreements. Are we going to pursue drama or pursue peace? Let's put it this way. To pursue peace puts you in agreement, even if you agree to disagree, much faster than drama.

Peace protects your energy while drama drains your energy.

CHAPTER 3

Words Matter

I am not a yeller or a fan of yelling. In fact, it actually creates instant tension in me because I presume the worst. I tend to think something terrible or horrific must have occurred or they would not be yelling.

Now, having said that, I also have to admit that we are not a quiet family, not by a long shot. However, we are also not an angry or mad family which I am so thankful for.

Many times in my counseling sessions I hear wives and husbands talk about how their spouse yells at them and the kids out of anger. It also seems that these angry yellers don't just yell at the biggest of things; they seem to yell any time they are upset. This is a very hurtful characteristic for spouses and children. The good news is, it's a habit and habits can be broken! It takes intentionality and focus, but anger and yelling can be conquered in a person's life.

So many times I have looked at someone in my office and said, "Please use your words, not your temper or emotional drama, to tell us you're angry." It takes way too much energy to yell, scream and be dramatic every time you're upset. Learning to use one's words to say you are angry is so much better for everyone involved than to show your anger through yelling and emotional outbursts.

Years ago I had an amazing and powerful vision. In the vision, I walked into this house of a family that I knew. I noticed that the dishes and china were all broken. In fact, the glass front of the hutch was broken as well. Also, as I walked around the house, I continued to see many other dishes and accessories that were broken. However, not one piece of furniture was broken. As I looked around the house in my vision, I asked the Lord what he was trying to show me. He then revealed to me that everything fragile in the house was broken.

Well, it was about to get very real because the house was only filled with girls. Girls are fragile, and these girls were broken. The father grew up in a house with only boys. This girl thing was new to him. He and his wife only had girls.

The Lord was showing me that the man in the house was too tough on his wife and daughters, and his anger and yelling were breaking them. He needed to make an immediate change if he didn't want his wife and daughters to be permanently broken and damaged.

If you are an angry yeller, learn to use your words to say you are angry. Use words versus volume and anger. Use words.

CHAPTER 4

Protect the Peace in Your Home

Chaos, drama, strife and division are way too draining to have in one's home where you should be able to have peace and recharge. Unfortunately, these emotionally draining atmospheres too often dominate in our homes.

There need to be boundaries and set standards on HOW one is going to express negative emotions in your home. Believe it or not, the way we deliver our feelings and emotions is a choice stemming from learned behavior. My experience as a marriage and family counselor has taught me that most don't consciously decide how they are going to express their emotions. Rather, they react with hurtful, childish and cutting words. Once spoken, words can't be taken back. Words shape relationships. Words are so impacting that it is of utmost necessity that we decide ahead of time how we will deliver our feelings. If we want to be heard the first time and want to build strong and peace-filled relationships, we must think before we speak.

Just last week I received a call. This person was full of drama and in a panic. She insisted that I return her call immediately. I received her message and quickly responded, but no answer. I called a few more times and again no answer. Twenty-four hours later she called me back with a trivial need, expecting me to give her information about someone. I then found out after she had left me that message that her phone had died and she did nothing to charge it. I very kindly, but firmly, educated her that drama is not the answer when handling drama. You must handle drama with peace, the peace of God.

Unfortunately, many people live with drama. As mature adults we must take control of our lives and not let the troubles of life take control of us.

It is vital to our mental, physical, spiritual and marital health and peace to protect the harmony and atmosphere of where we can love and recharge. Chaos is dysfunctional! We were not created to live in chaos and drama. In fact, years ago the Lord impressed upon me this statement, "Dysfunctional people destroy people." We all need peace to be at our very best; therefore, it is a must to protect the peace in your home.

CHAPTER 5

Ego

This chapter is a must for my book as it has been my experience that when the word ego is used, people think of it in the negative. But in fact, it is a positive word and is a need in the life of men for sure.

Although the word ego can have negative connotations, the word ego itself refers to a person's sense of self-esteem, self-importance, self-worth, self-image, and self-confidence. We all need a strong and positive ego to accomplish what we are called and responsible to do in our lifetime.

Let me tell you a story about myself. My amazing man and I are just finishing up our 33rd year of marriage. It didn't take me long to realize that I married a builder. He builds the church, people, marriages, families and even actual buildings. He loves to build! In fact, it's safe to say that if there has ever been a building project of any significance going up within an hour radius of us, we have watched the process of it being built!

This characteristic in him used to really challenge me, partly due to how big his thoughts and ideas were compared to what I had experienced. When he would share his ideas, my first response was to gulp! Then one day, after he shared an idea with me which I wasn't all that excited about, he said these words that I have never forgotten, "Cherrié, if you keep being negative about all my ideas, I'm going to stop sharing them with you." That's all he had to say. I knew enough to know that if he didn't share them with me, he would find someone else to share them with and I wasn't going to let that happen! It wasn't that I didn't think he could do them, I just hadn't yet learned how to dream.

I knew, even at the age of 20 when I married him, I knew that I knew, my man had greatness in him. Major greatness! When he would get discouraged and begin to question his own dreams, I would get upset and say to him, "I know who I married and I know you're called for greatness!" Every time I said this I fully meant it! I really did know at 20 years old that this hot, strong man of mine was called to do great things in life, and I am the fortunate one called to do it with him!

When Tim told me how important it was for me to believe in him and his dreams, I knew that I was called as his wife to build him up. I then understood how he and his ideas needed my encouragement, and I was the one called to be his cheerleader and build his ego. It's a man's ego that helps empower him to do all he is called to do. If my man didn't have a strong positive ego, self-worth, and a good self-esteem, why would he even try? Any simple hindrance, negative circumstance, or roadblock would stop him!

Hebrews 10:35 says, "Do not cast away your confidence as it will be greatly rewarded."

It is so very important, ladies, to protect and build your husband's ego so his confidence is strong and powerful. In fact, if he is to fulfill his dreams and visions in this life, it's a must!

CHAPTER 6

Custom Designed

Let me share with you how I discovered that marriages need to be custom designed.

Years ago, when my children were small, Tim came home one day and mentioned that he didn't like the toys so messy in the toy room. At the time, our downstairs family room didn't have any furniture in it so we designated it as the toy room.

I wasn't one to have toys all over the house. The toys were mainly in the toy room with a few exceptions where I allowed the kids to have a few toys in their rooms. The toys were never allowed to be all around the house in every room. However, this particular day when Tim came home, he expressed that he wanted them put away even more neatly. I thought that he was being too picky and thought to myself, "What's up with this? I have always kept a clean house." As usual, I went to the Lord to ask him to please explain to me this man He had given me! Lol

He clearly explained to me that He was putting a new level of excellence in Tim and I needed to rise up too. Well, there you go! I received my answer to my question and my direction for growth! It was time to go up again! Now, if I hadn't already submitted to the Lordship of

Jesus in our lives, I could have easily been insulted and offended by Tim. Instead I choose to go to His Maker and get my answer. I have always known my man was called for greatness, and I wanted to make sure I was qualified for it.

Here is my point, the Lord wants you to have a custom designed marriage, that is, a marriage which is being carved, sculpted, sketched, crafted, and molded by Him. Yes, this takes time, work and energy and mostly guidance from Him. Custom designed marriages can happen intentionally from both the wife and husband.

Jesus has a specific plan for your lives and legacy together. You were not made for mediocrity. You were designed for greatness and with a destiny.

It's vital that you not only try to be the best spouse you can be, but be the best spouse you can possibly be for who you are married to.

I know that I'm called by Tim's side and that means I need to grow with him and assure him that our kids grow with us. Our family is called to grow together and stay qualified for bigger and better things than what we see now. Tim likes to say, "Our best days are ahead", and they have been. I'm convinced they will continue to get bigger and better for the rest of our lives.

God wants you to receive the custom designed marriage He has for you.

CHAPTER 7

Set Me Up to Win
(I'm Not a Mind Reader)

"I can't read her mind." Wow, I wish I had a penny for every time I had a husband that said that to me in my office. I really don't think that wives want their husbands to read their minds. It's more like wives want their husbands to be mindful of them. Men, every once in a while, be spontaneous and bring her home a bouquet of flowers or perfume or whatever she likes. This says to her, "I was thinking of you today." This is so big to us wives by the way! Big points right there!

I know that my man has much on his mind and many decisions to make daily. I know he thinks of me because he stops by my office (right next to his) and calls me constantly throughout the day whether I'm at home or at another church campus. I also know that he is not thinking about my favorite perfume that is almost out. He is also not thinking, "Cherrié really could use a new pair of tan heels." He has no thoughts of these things unless I tell him. Ladies, hinting does not usually work for men. If you desire something, make it clear that it would be big points if he did this for you. Now, remember this isn't a demand or a sudden time line, but if he wanted to do something special for you, this is what he could do and

..an later would be great. Just know this, men do .ead minds.

The fact is there are times when every woman just needs a little something from her man. I call this helping her stay sweet.

Years ago I decided to help my man "win" with me when I needed something extra or just some pampering. So, for example, when my favorite perfume was out, I would ask him if he could stop by and buy me some new perfume. He would then let me know his schedule for the next few weeks and take my bottle and put it on his side of the closet island. This would help him remember to show his mindfulness of me and buy a new bottle.

Some women might say that because he didn't think of it on his own, it's not special. Well ladies, I know he has many things on his mind and that he also is not a mind reader. I decided a long time ago to use my words and let him know I could use something extra to make me feel special.

My husband so appreciates that I set him up to win with me. I appreciate that he wants to win with me! This little plan alone has done wonders for us.

CHAPTER 8

Cherish

Cherish, now there's a word we all know but probably don't use.

I would guess to say that most of us heard "to love and to cherish" in our wedding vows, but we don't think about the actions of cherishing.

What does cherish actually mean anyway? Cherish: to hold or treat as dear; feel love for; to care for tenderly; nurture; to cling fondly or inveterately.

It is clearly an act of adoration and love. To care for as a treasure.

A few weeks ago I asked both our congregations how many have used the word cherish in the last month? Not a hand was raised! That's exactly what I would have guessed. It just isn't a word or thought we tend to have, but yet we vowed to do it!

It's sad to see but there seems to be so many other loud things in our lives that take over our time and thoughts. We don't realize it at the time but it's so costly to our marriage, our spouse, our children, and even our life purpose when we don't actually take the time to show that we cherish our spouse. I wonder if we think it has to be some big planned-out event? The truth is, it doesn't.

It's many mindful acts of kindness and love that show we cherish our spouse. Just think how many that are divorced today would still be married if they had made acts of showing each other they are cherished. Just think of the example to our children or others around that would learn from these acts of kindness.

Remember, this isn't actually only a thought but it is a vow that we made to each other. A vow in front of the eyes of friends, family, and most of all, the Lord.

I'm willing to say that the truth is we need to learn HOW to cherish our spouse.

The best person to ask is actually your spouse. We all know what doesn't make us feel cherished, cared for or appreciated. We tend to be quick to communicate that to our spouse, but even more importantly our spouse needs to know WHAT they do or can do to make us feel admired, honored and a treasure. Yes, we need to use words and share with our spouse what makes us feel loved and embraced.

As I meet with couples and ask them if they actually share with each other what makes them feel like a treasure to their spouse, they look at me like I'm a foreigner! They have never talked like this with each other! It's a completely new thought!

Eph. 5:33 in the Bible says that a husband is to love his wife as Christ loved the church and a wife is to honor her husband.

This scripture is directive and powerful, but I have only had a few people actually stop and think about what this means.

What does this mean? Of course, we know that Christ loves the church. Yes, we know that a husband is to love his wife. The real question here is, what does that look like and how should he act to show his wife this?

This clearly doesn't just happen. Hopefully you had a good example in your life of what this looks like, but like myself many of us didn't have that privilege. I can personally think of one example of a great marriage that I saw when I was growing up. It was my Aunt JoAnn and Uncle Harry. Yes, they bickered but they did more in a teasing manner and were inseparable! They loved each other dearly and everyone knew it! But even then, I didn't live with them. It wasn't a daily view for me to "catch" without thinking!

As I have counseled so many couples, I have found that most are like myself. They just didn't have a good example; therefore, their understanding of a great marriage is weak.

The good news is you can still have a great marriage but it must be intentional. With all the books and you-tube teachings today, you can have a great marriage if you both want it and have an ear to hear each other.

As I meet with couples, I often ask them how their spouse feels loved and honored, that is, what acts they do that make them feel this way. THIS IS NOT A SET-UP OR TRICK QUESTION! This is vital to know! The usual response is vague or obvious but not necessarily personal or realized how important these acts or affirmations are to them. The reality is these are life givers to our spouse. These acts that make each other feel loved and cherished keep us healthy and connected. They help keep us in a place to grow together.

A woman wants/needs to feel loved. A man needs/ wants to feel honored. I want to encourage you to ask your spouse, even today, what you can do to make them feel honored and loved.

CHAPTER 9

The Power of Touch

This has been such a huge key for us, especially when we have gone through adversity. When you're hurting, you can so quickly feel empty. The fact is adversity is real and a part of life. It is vital to think right, and intentionally work to be healthy.

Proverbs 24:10 says that "if you faint in the day of adversity your strength is small."

The point here is don't let your strength become weak. Stay strong, and a key for us personally has been to simply touch each other. Hold hands even when you are exhausted and empty after a long day of working hard.

I can specifically remember a season when we were going through a very tough time. Our older kids were in high school, and we were just trying to hold one of our campuses together due to betrayal and division from the leadership team.

Our older three kids were in varsity sports and we went to everything.

There were many times that we felt empty, hurt and exhausted. So as we were watching the games, we would just hold hands and cheer on our kids. We received positive comments from parents that were always touching, and our kids received comments from other kids that their parents were always holding hands. It's true. Little did they know that we not only were holding hands because we like each other, but we were holding hands to "recharge" each other. We needed to connect to build energy. There is so much power and energy given just by simply touching.

Chapter 10

Repent and Initiate

I found myself wrestling with the Lord, thinking to myself I must be crazy with all the thoughts that permeated my mind. Doing my best to listen to my man as he was preaching, the only thought I could hear was: 'Repent and Initiate'.

Finally realizing the Lord was speaking to me, I asked for more. I felt that He was saying there are many wives who have rarely, or perhaps never, initiated intimacy with their husband. The message this lack of initiative sends to their husband is that they were not 'wanted' by their wife.

I felt the mandate to teach women (wives) that when they initiate intimacy, the male ego is fed. This is of vital importance in the institution of marriage. Our men need, and want, to know that they are desired by their wives.

As I wrestled with these thoughts, I could not help but also reflect on the realization that this is a church service and the timing of such thoughts was not appropriate. Funny, right?! Imagine the Lord teaching such things during a church service, how dare He! This may sound silly, but these were my thoughts.

As Tim finished his messages, he looked at me and said: "Honey, do you have something to share?" (My man knows me well.) I hesitated, but I knew I had something to share. With a bit of slight hesitancy, I stood up and delivered exactly what the Lord had been bombarding my thoughts with during the service, and I shared why. The words flowed easily: "If you are the spouse that rarely, or never initiates, then you need to REPENT AND INITIATE!" I also mentioned that I suspected the church would 'clear out' after service very quickly that day. It's important to have fun in church.

I must also point out the fact that it isn't always the wife who doesn't 'initiate'; some men are at fault as well. There are some marital unions where the husbands do not possess a strong sexual interest, even though this is not as common.

The response that morning, after I had shared what the Lord had been speaking to me, was GRATITUDE... (Albeit more so from the men than the women). Most of the women simply just 'looked' at me as if their husbands must have had a private conversation with me. It was clear, by the responses of our congregation, that this was a much needed and timely word.

As I left the sanctuary that morning to travel to the service at our other campus in Minneapolis, a gentleman in his late 70's chased me down to say, "Thank you! That was a great word and well needed."

I decided a long time ago that the Lord can use our pulpit and platform to share anything with our people to help them grow AND have great marriages! I was not fully aware, at the time, that I would be the one He would use to share on such topics. I truly love seeing marriages change and the overwhelming happiness that change brings into their homes. I am passionately pursuing my commission to educate people on how to have a great marriage.

CHAPTER 11

Use Your Words

I really have no idea how many times I have been counseling a couple and anger shows up so easily. The lack of using words instead of anger or threats is actually very sad to me. I can't actually remember when or whom I first looked at and said, "Use words instead of emotions", but it appears like a new thought to the person whenever I say it.

Here's the deal, sure we can shout, scream and have a temper tantrum, but why make ourselves look foolish? How crazy is that?! Words matter, and how they are said matters too!

Many times I'll look at someone and say it's better to say you're angry instead of showing that you're angry. Why not just communicate how you're feeling instead of showing everyone how you're feeling?

When Tim and I were newlyweds, he "made" me learn how to communicate. Yes, I mean made me, and I'm very thankful he did.

Tim had pastored as a handsome, hot (it's my book!) single man for over six years when we had met. He saw that it was very important to learn how to communicate, not only with his sermons but with everything! I was only a young twenty-year old and really had no clue how to communicate! I was very good (for awhile) to just be quiet and be the peacemaker by stuffing feelings. We all know how that works, with every stuffer eventually comes an explosion! So, for the first few years of our marriage, about every six months his sweet wife (that's me) would explode. This is when he would wonder what was happening to his wife! I'm guessing many of you understand this scene! Because I was not a good communicator, that led me to be a "runner!"

When we would argue or when I couldn't contain my lists of hurts anymore, I would typically head out the door for a run or take the car and just get away! (Never any place to go!)

However, one day my man decided to grab my keys first and told me we are going to have a great marriage, and that meant we needed to sit down and discuss our disagreements! Discuss what? What the heck does that look like? What does that mean?

The only thing I agreed with when he would say that, was that I wanted a great marriage, I just didn't know how to get there. So, I sat down in our dining room and tried to talk. Such a foreign thought, let alone an act for me. The only thing going for me in that moment was that I had self-awareness of my limitations. There were many in this area. Yikes! First, I had no example! Secondly, that took energy!

The truth is, as I am writing this now, I vividly remember the exhaustion that I felt trying to learn how to communicate in a mature manner, how I was feeling. Oh, to put words to my feelings! Wow! Or should I say "ouch".

On several occasions I remember looking at Tim and saying, "I am not mature enough right now to finish this conversation!" I also would assure him that I too wanted a great marriage, and I needed a little break to go for a run or walk and "find" some maturity and come back and finish the conversation. He seemed to understand that and was ok with it. So, I would do just that. I'd go for a run or walk and get the right words to express how I was feeling and come back and finish our conversation maturely.

Yes, I really do remember the exhaustion of learning how to communicate, and yes, I remember the feeling of maturity and being proud of myself when we completed the conversation. It's work, but oh, so worth it and an absolute must in order to have a great marriage.

CHAPTER 12

He Who Finds a Good Wife

He who finds a wife finds a good thing,
and obtains favor from the Lord.

Proverbs 18:22

Now let's think about that scripture. How do you find a wife? If you find a wife, doesn't that mean you have found someone else's wife? After all, she is a wife.

No! This scripture isn't talking about someone already married. It's talking about a woman that already has the heart of a wife. Her desire is to be the helper of a man and become one with the vision and plan for them together.

The scripture goes on to say that he finds a good thing and obtains (receives) favor from the Lord.

A woman that has a selfless heart to be a wife to her husband is a blessing to her husband. She is a force to help create increase for him which also means to herself and her family.

She brings peace and love and works to create an atmosphere of dreaming, healing and love. This is an atmosphere where dreaming can happen!

A wife needs to learn how to be a wife to the man she married as well as the man needs to learn how to be a husband to the wife he married.

I so wish every man and woman fully understood the verses about marriage. It's very clear that it takes intention to understand how to live well and have a life of blessings.

CHAPTER 13

A Woman Is Like a Horse

Before I delve into this chapter, I must ask the ladies to simply trust me. In my counsel to many couples, I have used this analogy of 'a woman is like a horse' with men to help them understand their wives. I have shared these things on international platforms, and the men 'get it' – they love it.

In the genesis of unfolding this analogy, I ask the men how many know anything about horses, or have even spent any time around them. Always a few respond in the affirmative, while most others look at me with bewilderment, wondering where in the world I could possibly be going with this!

Continuing, I relay to the men that you do not randomly approach a horse, but gradually advance towards her, as she needs to first decide if she can trust you. Extending your hand, the horse sniffs it, checking you out. The horse, not you, decides if she wants to get closer. If the animal approves, you can then get closer to touch and feed her, all the while the horse is checking you out to see if you can be trusted. It is all about trust. IF a horse cannot trust you – she will nag, shake her head, dig her hooves into the ground, and stubbornness will prevail... and IF you are able to mount this horse, your ride is destined to be very brief as you are about to be 'thrown off' of her.

If the horse decides you can be trusted, you can then saddle her, ride her, and even nudge the horse to make her go faster. It is 'all good', because the horse 'trusts' you! Earning her trust is the prerequisite!

Building this analogy, either to the large audience I stand before, or the lone gentleman sitting in my office, I finally just make it plain: "A WOMAN IS LIKE A HORSE!" Then my attention goes immediately to the wife, and I reassure her that she can trust me.

Husbands, your lady needs you to be gentle. As you show patience, care, and prove yourself to be trustworthy, you can then urge her along to run with you at an even faster pace in your pursuit of purpose together. Then I drop this line: "If you have earned the trust of your lady, she will then let you get on and ride her!" This usually brings a blushing moment and a look of shock upon the listeners. In international meetings, this moment of my message always brings my interpreter to fumble for the words to translate, as he blushes from embarrassment. The crowd always bursts into laughter AND the wives clap and cheer as they realize their man – GOT IT!

Remember, the goal here is to have a great marriage in all areas.

CHAPTER 14

When We Are in Our 80's

From the outset of our marriage of more than 33 years, I have heard my husband make this declaration: "When we are in our 80's…"

Tim has taught me to think 'backwards' (or to begin with the end in mind) in life. What does this mean? My man finishes this statement in two different ways. First he says: "When we are in our 80's it is vital to me that you do not have any regrets that you married me." For the last 33 plus years of marriage together he has shown me the imperative importance of his heart in these regards.

On a regular basis he has come to me to 'check in' on how he is doing in this stance. He reminds me of his lifelong goal to make this more than merely a statement, but a reality. This means more to me than he even realizes; it is special and makes me feel cherished. He keeps this as a lifelong goal.

When I am 80, will I look back and be proud of what I am and the example I have been? Will I stand in my twilight years and look back over my life and be proud of the precedent I set forth in my children's and grandkids' lives?

The sum of that statement will make you think differently and live purposely to pursue life productively. This thought alone will continue to give you direction into destiny – knowing that we are a 'lifetime' couple.

In your mind you may be thinking 'OF COURSE'! On the other hand, you may be thinking this is a completely new thought as you are just hoping to make it through the day and see tomorrow's daybreak.

We all would like to believe that everyone thinks 'lifetime' is settled. The divorce rate obviously presents a different scenario.

When my husband says these things to me, he often has tears in his eyes. He looks deep into my eyes to hear and see my reaction. This is always amazing to me; it is even sexy leadership!

Leadership offers direction to our marriage, family, and legacy. This initiative says, "I want to make sure you think I am a great husband." – I DO!

CHAPTER 15

Redo

'Redo' – this is a common practice between me and my man. Actually as this new day dawns, we have been married for almost 33 years!

Here is the setting:

We are on vacation in Mexico. While Tim was finishing a chapter on his new book, I headed down early to breakfast. With phone in hand I began to check some of my current e-mails, and shortly thereafter he arrived.

As I was finishing scanning through my e-mails, Tim said to me: "Did you invite me to have breakfast to talk or to watch you enamored with what is on your phone?" I looked at him and said: "You just arrived, and I am finishing up an e-mail; please don't be rude."

I could tell he was impatient, and he could tell I was annoyed at his rudeness. This was a defining moment – we could either be ticked and spoil the day OR we could use a 'REDO' and enjoy breakfast and the day together. Thankfully we chose 'REDO' and we proceeded with our breakfast, conversation, and laughter which set the course for the day!

In all fairness I credit Tim for granting me a 'redo'. After all, I'm sure I have plenty in reserve, for when I asked for a 'redo' – he did – all was right. It will serve us well if we are quick to say yes and make a fresh start of the conversation or day. This takes a conscious decision and effort, but the payoff is so worth it.

We are all privy to the moments when a conversation starts out on a bad path. Perhaps you may be focused on something and deep in thought when someone rushes into the room needing something NOW! At that moment you are invested in a conversation in your head rather than taking a pause. At the rude interruption you snap back with an unpleasant retort. A moment like this is the perfect opportunity to ask: "Can I have a redo?"

For those in a second marriage or new relationship, and you respond to the new out of habit from the old, this is seldom fruitful. Your new spouse (relationship) is NOT your old spouse (relationship). This is a new day dawning and this relationship deserves a fresh start and a new level of communication. This is reality – when one relationship comes to an end, communication is at its worst. Unless there is an intentional change and healing from the past one, it is futile. A new start can be rough.

"Can I have a redo?" is a tremendous method to use when you are in the fray of new/old. You and your partner are breaking old habits and embarking on something new – something God. We are all human. This realization can catapult us to jump on the right path for positive conversation and future.

CHAPTER 16

Lover

The difference is vast between 'having sex' and being intimate. After decades of doing marriage counseling it has become quite clear to me that both men and women desire a 'lover' as opposed to simply having someone to have sex with. Being a 'lover' is a completely different experience to merely having a sex partner. Often, quite sadly, in my sessions with women they feel (and speak) like the act of love-making in their marriage is as if they were doing their husband a 'favor'. Surprisingly, some men feel the same.

Ladies, bear with me and hear with your heart. I can't imagine the Lord creating the gift of intimacy for only just one of the persons in this union. This act of marriage is a time where both the husband and wife can be vulnerable, transparent, and literally naked before each other in a matter of trust that is unveiled by sacred love. This is a closeness that you have with only one person on the planet. It is a different kind of relationship with your spouse that no one else is to be privy to.

In our modern day we are subjugated by so much information that is only one 'Google' away, yet brokenness in marriages and relationships has reached epidemic proportions. WHY? Why has the divorce rate in America soared to all-time highs? Why has the family structure become so complex?

These may be 'loaded' questions, but they stand deserving an answer. I am of the persuasion it all begins with the leadership and vision in the church. The husband and wife union is the lead in the family structure. When mom and dad are solid together at the core, it creates a healthy strong launching pad for the children to have security and grow.

It truly saddens me to watch our culture today 'dumb down' marriage, lifelong relationships, and unions – yet all the while this is everyone's dream. It takes intention and work to have a great marriage. It takes teaching, coaching, and understanding to build a marriage that heaven inaugurated. It will require continuing education and communication as both parties change and adapt thoughts, patterns, and the processing of goals as time passes. Just when you think you are in a routine, life can change.

It is not out of the ordinary for either Tim or me to start a dialogue with "I made a decision today." When this proclamation is trumpeted, it means one of two things. One – that I changed my thinking about something in my life. Two – we are asking the other about our thoughts to make sure they are healthy thoughts/decisions that keep us steered in the right direction.

Regardless of the issues you face – health, past pornography, rape, or whatever hurt that haunts your heart – you must know that Jesus can heal you and you can enjoy the intimacy with your spouse that heaven ordained.

CHAPTER 17

Gargoyles

Years ago Tim and I were driving in Tulsa to join some friends for dinner. With Tim at the wheel, my eyes caught a sight I will never forget! I actually could not believe what my eyes beheld.

In front of our car I saw two gargoyle-looking creatures cross the road in front of us. Looking to bring a confirmation to this sight, I asked Tim if he too could see them. "No", he responded. It was surreal and strange, but vivid. I know what I saw was in the spiritual realm, but at that moment the understanding of what I had seen eluded me.

At that moment I inquired of the Lord as to the meaning of what my eyes were opened to. The words 'seeking whom they may devour' immediately came to my spirit. When those words came to me, I looked to see where these imps had pilgrimaged from and where their targeted destination was. It was across the street to another residential subdivision.

Suddenly I was made aware that these ugly creatures were on assignment to a nearby family who were engulfed in a two-way selfish disagreement where the initial tone was acceptable. These demonic creatures were sent to escalate the argument into an all-out explosion where words are spoken in haste, regretted in the many days to come – disagreements turned into division as the subtle onslaught pushes to divide and conquer this holy union between husband and wife.

Let me pose this question to you: Have you ever had a simple disagreement in the beginning turn into a horrific memory at its conclusion? Words were spoken that continue to echo in your mind because of the inflicted pain. Have you ever contemplated, after the fact, as to how/why such a meager matter took such a terrible turn? How did it happen? What just happened? We have all experienced this ugliness.

The brief few seconds of this vision unveiled so much to my spirit. I was fully cognizant that there are spiritual beings, who are issued an order from the kingdom of darkness and sent to destroy that which God ordained.

> Be well balanced and always alert, because your enemy, the devil, roams around incessantly, like a roaring lion looking for its prey to devour.

1 Peter 5:8 Passion Translation

At that moment, this familiar portion of Scripture became more of a reality than ever before.

We read: "Be sober (self-controlled), be vigilant (watchful); your adversary (demons) are walking about to see whom they may devour (may next wreak havoc upon)." The word 'devour' here carries much weight; it is total destruction! We must NOT be ignorant of Satan and his designed devices – he wants to destroy marriages and families!

We all have disagreements; such is part of being human and living life. We must also be aware, informed, and alert as to the ploys of the enemy. You can disagree in a healthy and productive way, but you can also disagree in a wrong and destructive manner. Keep your emotions under control and your tongue from being a destructive force, even in the midst of disagreements. Protect your marriage, your spouse, and your family. We have an enemy – be alert, be protective – and as you do, be ready for amazing results in your marriage.

CHAPTER 18

Forgiveness

Forgiveness is a word that is rarely recited as part of the vows of a wedding ceremony; however, it must be a living/vibrant part of the marriage.

As two people embark upon their new life together, living under the same roof and being involved in virtually every aspect of each other's lives, there will inevitably be times when offense or disappointments will arise. When these times arise, FORGIVENESS must be quickly afforded.

After three decades of pastoring and counseling, I have concluded that forgiveness and letting go of grudges is one of the biggest factors in marriages that are strong! Ladies, let me put it to you like this: Forgiveness is the best skin care, anti-aging product on the market! It was costly as Jesus paid a dear price for it – and then made it free for us! Unforgiveness on the face of a lady is very unattractive. Unforgiveness is the worst thing we can do to ourselves, both inside and out.

I remember as a child rationalizing to myself: "I don't need to forgive anyone until they ask for forgiveness." As I grew older and wiser, I realized that forgiveness was a gift for me. Unforgiveness was a burden that I did not have to bear, and it was my choice to lay it down and not harbor it in my heart. However, trust is completely different.

As I counsel it is very clear to me that most cannot distinguish the difference between forgiveness and trust. Most think that if they forgive the offense, they have to now 'trust' the offender. This is simply not true. Forgiveness and trust have two totally different definitions with two totally different courses of action.

We need to forgive so we can free ourselves from carrying that baggage, a weight that our spirit was never designed to carry. Trust, on the other hand, is something that the offender must earn back. Forgiving is the best thing you can do for yourself and all of your relationships.

CHAPTER 19

Beware of the Promiscuous Woman

Follow my advice, my son; always treasure my commands. ² Obey my commands and live! Guard my instructions as you guard your own eyes. ³ Tie them on your fingers as a reminder. Write them deep within your heart. ⁴ Love wisdom like a sister; make insight a beloved member of your family. ⁵ Let them protect you from an affair with an immoral woman, from listening to the flattery of a promiscuous woman. ⁶ While I was at the window of my house, looking through the curtain, ⁷ I saw some naive young men, and one in particular who lacked common sense. ⁸ He was crossing the street near the house of an immoral woman, strolling down the path by her house. ⁹ It was at twilight, in the evening, as deep darkness fell. ¹⁰ The woman approached him, seductively dressed and sly of heart. ¹¹ She was the brash, rebellious type, never content to stay at home. ¹² She is often in the streets and markets, soliciting at every corner.

[13] She threw her arms around him and kissed him, and with a brazen look she said, [14] "I've just made my peace offerings and fulfilled my vows. [15] You're the one I was looking for! I came out to find you, and here you are! [16] My bed is spread with beautiful blankets, with colored sheets of Egyptian linen. [17] I've perfumed my bed with myrrh, aloes, and cinnamon. [18] Come, let's drink our fill of love until morning. Let's enjoy each other's caresses, [19] for my husband is not home. He's away on a long trip. [20] He has taken a wallet full of money with him and won't return until later this month." [21] So she seduced him with her pretty speech and enticed him with her flattery. [22] He followed her at once, like an ox going to the slaughter. He was like a stag caught in a trap, [23] awaiting the arrow that would pierce its heart. He was like a bird flying into a snare, little knowing it would cost him his life. [24] So listen to me, my sons, and pay attention to my words. [25] Don't let your hearts stray away toward her. Don't wander down her wayward path. [26] For she has been the ruin of many; many men have been her victims. [27] Her house is the road to the grave. Her bedroom is the den of death.

Proverbs 7:1-27
New Living Translation

Our arch enemy Satan, the devil, hates marriages and knows the power of a strong marriage and what a couple can accomplish together when they are in unity. Therefore, husbands and wives must be aware of his tactics against them and this marriage union.

The author of Proverbs chapter 7 warns couples concerning one of these tactics of the enemy, the promiscuous woman. He describes her as immoral, seductive, sly of heart, brash, rebellious, brazen, and full of flattery. Her target is the strong man who has been wounded in his journey of life. Proverbs 7:26 in the King James Version of the Bible says:

"For she has cast down many wounded. All
who were slain by her were strong men."

Women, and not just immoral or promiscuous women, are attracted to strong men. Strong men are attractive! Yet when the scriptures speak of strong men their reference isn't just to the physique of a man, but they refer to a man who exudes vision, confidence, focus, drive and productivity.

Strong men become vulnerable when they have become wounded. Life is not always easy and it entails many battles and conflicts. Strong men and their wives need to protect themselves and each other from becoming permanently wounded, broken in spirit and soul.

Wives, no one can better minister to your husband than you. He needs your love, encouragement and belief in him to stay strong and heal from life's inevitable wounds. Ladies, men have a God-given ego with the need for his ego to be stroked and built up. He desires your attention and has a need for it in his life. The promiscuous woman understands this need in his life and is more than willing to give him the attention he needs. Wise wives feed their husband's egos (not tear them down) and give them the attention they so need and desire.

Ladies, let your man know that you love him, are happy you married him, and want to be a good wife to him. Men, the same goes for you. Your wife needs to know you feel the same way about her.

Men, it is equally important for you to communicate with your wife (and vice versa, of course) what you have need of and what is your love language. Communication is perhaps the biggest need of any marriage if it is going to be one of quality.

The writer of Proverbs lets us know how vitally important it is for a married couple to understand the potential danger of the promiscuous woman to their marriage. Her goal is to seduce the strong man away from his marriage vows and destroy his marriage and family. The New Century Version says, "She has ruined many good men..."

She not only destroys marriages and families but she also steals the strength of the strong man, his vision, confidence and authority in the process. The New King James Version translation says that this kind of woman will reduce the strong man "to a crust of bread." She may cost him everything, including his very life. The Easy to Read Version translation says, "She has brought down some of the most powerful men; she has left many dead bodies in her path."

It is vitally important for husbands and wives to listen to one another, take care of each other's needs, and protect the gift of marriage that God has given to them as a couple.

CHAPTER 20

Decisions You Control

Here I was, at only 25 years old, and my new office was open for counseling at the church. A lady in her 60's came in for counseling. She had family in our church; however, she did not attend herself. Anger and regrets and a multitude of issues were her constant companions throughout her everyday life. Because of her family who were attending our church, I knew she was harsh to her kids, cruel to her stepchild, and simply just an angry woman.

When she departed from my office that day, I was compelled to make a decision that has never left me, a decision that has guided many of my decisions in life to this very day. My decision: 'I was never going to let hatred take up residency inside of me. I was always going to be a loving person all of my days. I would never walk hand in hand with bitterness but stroll through ALL of my life with forgiveness and love.' I decided right then and there, as a 25-year-old, who and what I was going to be in my 30's, 40's, 50's, 60's, and beyond!

At that moment in time, even though I didn't realize it, my course was set. My road map was made clear. It was a decision that governed many future verdicts for me that have served me well. That one decision dictated how I would handle future offenses, hurts, betrayals, and disappointments. That one decision was a turning point – a faith foundation – that has protected my heart.

Marriage can be very much the same way. Of course, it takes both parties to decide how your marriage is going to be, but this decision is a crucial one, and a decision worth keeping at the helm of your relationship.

We are all aware that 'life happens', and when it does, we will find ourselves in a place where we have to decide together how we are going to respond. Decide AHEAD OF TIME that your marriage is going to be great. Put in place a plan to protect your vision and the best decision for your marriage. Put Jesus and the Word of God first place in your life and marriage relationship.

Have a meeting and plan a vision for your marriage, family, and future. Your decision will be your road map for all the other decisions you will need to make in your future. Great marriages are made intentionally!

Biography

Cherrié Peterson has been married to Dr. Tim Peterson for 33 years. They have four children, Trey, Rachelle, Chantel and Trom. They also have two grandchildren, Cyrus and Taytum, from Trey and his wife Stephany. Cherrié absolutely loves being a woman, wife, mom and now a grandmother, and has greatly enjoyed every season.

Cherrié has a passion and heart to see couples learn how to have great marriages, the kind of marriages that brings a high standard of love and respect to the powerful union of marriage. She has spent the last 28 years counseling marriages and families and has come to believe that most couples just "wing it" and hope it all turns out ok.

Cherrié has had the honor and excitement of helping many marriages and families learn the *"how to"* of a great life together. Her desire is to continue to help couples learn about their spouse and how powerful they can be together.

My honorary doctorate graduation from Life Christian University in Florida.

Christmas 2019.

My men enjoying one of our many hobbies on Lake Minnetonka, MN. We spend a lot of time on the boat as a family.

The next generation begins with Cyrus Conrad Peterson 6-2-2017.

The Peterson family. Picture taken in 2018.

When I walk into a room, I've learned to listen for his laugh rather than to look for him. So thankful for the joy he carries!

Thirty-three years and going strong. I'm so in love with "my man".

We often preach together.

July 25th, 1987. I was only 20 years old and now a pastor's wife! Oh, I had much to learn quickly!

Tim and our youngest, Trom.

Trip to Uganda in 2020. I visited Pastors Timothy and Janepher Kakooza and their amazing ministry at Winners Children's Home.

I absolutely adore my man!

My beautiful granddaughter Taytum.

Owatonna Campus.

Edina Campus.

The beginning of our Southern MN Prayer Garden.
This is a sculpture created by Artist Max Greiner.

Books written by Dr. Cherrié Peterson

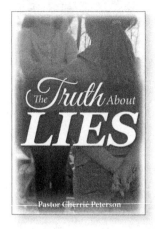

available at

amazon

Made in the USA
Monee, IL
23 January 2021